Thomas Edison

History Maker Bios

Shannon Zemlicka

⌐ LERNER PUBLICATIONS COMPANY • MINNEAPOLIS

For my nephew Luke, another boy with a healthy dose of curiosity

Illustrations by Tim Parlin

Text copyright © 2004 by Lerner Publications Company
Illustrations copyright © 2004 by Lerner Publications Company

Lerner Publications Company
A division of Lerner Publishing Group
241 First Avenue North
Minneapolis, MN 55401 U.S.A.

Website address: www.lernerbooks.com

Library of Congress Cataloging-in-Publication Data

Zemlicka, Shannon.
    Thomas Edison / by Shannon Zemlicka.
        p. cm. — (History maker bios)
    Summary: An introduction to the life of Thomas Edison, who invented the
light bulb, the phonograph, and moving pictures.
    Includes bibliographical references and index.
    ISBN 0-8225-0239-9 (lib. bdg.)
    1. Edison, Thomas A. (Thomas Alva), 1847–1931—Juvenile literature.
2. Inventors—United States—Biography—Juvenile literature. [1.
Edison, Thomas A. (Thomas Alva), 1847–1931. 2. Inventors.] I. Title.
II. Series.
    TK140.E3 Z46 2003
621.3'092--dc21   2002152937

Manufactured in the United States of America
1 2 3 4 5 6 – JR – 09 08 07 06 05 04

TABLE OF CONTENTS

INTRODUCTION

Thomas Edison was one of the greatest inventors of all time. His creations changed the way people lived, communicated, and had fun.

Edison's first famous invention helped make the telephone work better. Then, in 1877, he built the phonograph, a machine that could record and play back sound. Soon after, his lightbulb brought electric light to the world. Later he made the first machine that could create and show movies.

As a boy, Edison hardly went to school. When he did, he wasn't a very good student. But he was curious about the world around him and willing to work hard. As a result, he did amazing things.

This is his story.

1 A Curious Boy

Young Thomas Edison was nicknamed Al—short for his middle name, Alva. Al hated school. Day after day, he tried to memorize his lessons at the one-room schoolhouse in Port Huron, Ohio. But repeating the same facts over and over was the most boring thing that he could imagine.

To make matters worse, Al was partly deaf and had a hard time hearing his teacher. He tended to get sick often, too. Life had been hard on many of the Edison children. Three of Al's six older brothers and sisters had died before his birth in 1847.

Al struggled through a few months of school. Then his mother, Nancy, decided to teach him herself at home. Al had always loved to read. Now he could read books about history and science instead of trying to repeat lessons he couldn't hear.

Al was eight when he posed for this photograph with his older sister Harriet Ann.

Learning at home gave Al more time to explore Port Huron, too. He especially liked to watch machines at work. At the telegraph office, operators tapped keys to send messages along wires to other towns. The messages traveled in Morse code, a system of dots and dashes that stood for letters.

Then there was the railroad. All over the United States, miles of new railroad track were connecting towns. In 1859, the tracks reached Port Huron.

These tourists are enjoying an unusual ride on the front of a train engine. Railroad tracks were being laid all over the United States so that travelers could reach many towns and cities by train.

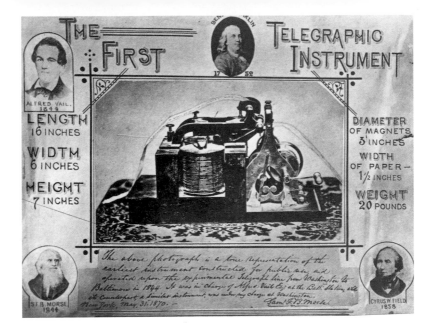

Samuel Morse invented the telegraph, which was a way of sending messages over electric wires.

Al studied the trains every chance he had. The turning of the wheels and the hissing of the powerful steam engines amazed him.

Wherever he went, his mind filled with questions. How did steam make a train move? How did telegraph wires carry messages? With a little help from his books, he built a model train and stretched a telegraph line between his house and a friend's. He even started teaching himself Morse code.

Al went to work selling candy and newspapers on the local train when he was twelve years old.

Al's interest in trains led him to take a job on one. At age twelve, he became a news butch. His job was to sell newspapers and snacks to passengers as the train rolled from Port Huron to Detroit and back again.

Al worked hard, but he had energy to spare. In between his sales on the train, he did chemistry experiments in an empty baggage car.

In 1862, Al turned fifteen. Almost a grown man, he started going by Tom, short for Thomas. He had a new goal—to become a telegraph operator. He started to spend more time in the telegraph offices on his train route.

Most offices had several telegraphs. The sounds of their clicking filled the room as operators sent and received messages. For once, Tom's hearing problem helped him. When he sat down at a telegraph, all he could hear was the machine in front of him. The noises of the others didn't disturb him.

Mount Clemens was one of the railroad stations on Tom's route that had a telegraph office.

Tom spent hour after hour learning to take down messages quickly. He quit his train job to work in Port Huron's telegraph office. Then a better job opened up in a small town in Ontario, Canada. Tom left home to seek his fortune there.

After that, he moved from city to city, working at telegraph offices at night and reading books by day. He usually slept just a few hours a day.

A LUCKY LEAP

A famous story tells how Tom's quick thinking got him into the telegraph business. One day, Tom saw a little boy playing on the tracks at a station near Detroit. The boy was the stationmaster's son—and a freight train was heading right for him! Tom leaped onto the tracks and snatched the boy out of harm's way as the train rushed by. The grateful stationmaster offered to give Tom telegraph lessons.

As Tom learned more about telegraphs, he began to tinker with gadgets to make them work better. As much as he liked operating telegraphs, taking them apart to see how they worked was even more fun.

When Tom was twenty, he got a new operator job in Boston. There he began to work on a new idea. He built an electric vote recorder. This machine could keep track of how lawmakers voted on new laws.

There was one problem with Tom's invention. No one wanted to buy an electric vote recorder. Tom's idea was clever but not very useful.

This failure didn't discourage him. He had found his true calling. In 1869, he quit his telegraph job. From now on, he would spend all his time inventing.

Tom's first invention was the vote recorder, but lawmakers didn't care for it.

2 YOUNG INVENTOR

The first thing Edison learned about inventing was that it wasn't cheap. He needed money to buy materials and to support himself. He raised funds from business owners who wanted to sell the things he invented.

For a while, he kept working on ideas to improve the telegraph. Then, in 1870, he opened an inventing shop in Newark, New Jersey. There, dozens of workers built machines based on his ideas.

Edison worked harder than he ever had. On some days, he spent nineteen hours in the shop. He was just twenty-three years old, but his hair began to turn white. He liked his work too much to mind.

Edison opened an inventing shop in Newark, New Jersey, in 1870.

The next year, he met a friendly, pretty young woman named Mary Stilwell. She worked at a telegraph service Edison had started. He was ready to settle down, and Mary seemed like the right girl for him. They married on Christmas Day of 1871.

The couple's first child, Marion, was born in 1873. Edison gave the little girl a nickname that reminded him of the Morse code he enjoyed using so much. He called her Dot.

Mary Stilwell worked in Tom's office. He married her in 1871.

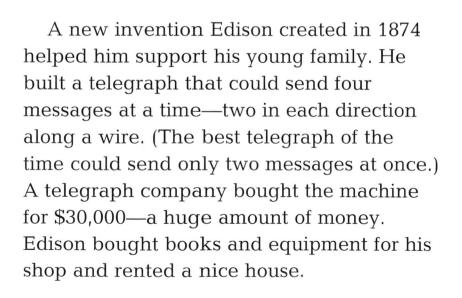

Marion Edison, Tom's daughter, was eight years old when this photograph was taken.

A new invention Edison created in 1874 helped him support his young family. He built a telegraph that could send four messages at a time—two in each direction along a wire. (The best telegraph of the time could send only two messages at once.) A telegraph company bought the machine for $30,000—a huge amount of money. Edison bought books and equipment for his shop and rented a nice house.

Mary Edison is standing on the front porch of the Edisons' new home in Menlo Park, New Jersey.

He didn't spend much time in the new house. It seemed impossible to sit chatting in Mary's fancy parlor when there were experiments to be done and machines to be built. Once a new question entered his head, he couldn't let it go until he had worked out the next step in answering it. Some nights, he didn't come home from the shop at all.

One idea that kept Edison busy was the telephone. Several inventors were racing to build a machine that would make it possible for people to talk over a long distance. Edison hoped to be the first to succeed.

While he worked on this project, Mary gave birth to a son, Thomas Alva Jr., in January 1876. Tom nicknamed him Dash.

Edison's growing family and business needed more space. He bought a house and some land in the little town of Menlo Park, New Jersey. There he built a new laboratory. It was a true invention factory, filled with tools, machines, chemicals, and books.

Edison's invention factory was one block from his home in Menlo Park. His workers gathered on the balcony and the front porch to have their picture taken.

As the family moved to Menlo Park, another bright thinker beat Edison to the invention of the telephone. Alexander Graham Bell created a working telephone in March 1876. For the first time, people could talk back and forth along a wire instead of sending telegraph messages or letters.

Bell's telephone wasn't perfect. A person had to shout into it to be heard at the other end. And a message could be carried only a short distance.

Alexander Graham Bell invented the telephone, but Edison wanted to make it work better.

MORE ABOUT MENLO PARK

Edison's laboratory had everything he needed to explore his many ideas. Shelves held more than 2,500 bottles of chemicals for experiments. There was a steam engine, a darkroom for developing photographs, and plenty of telegraph and telephone equipment. There was even a person-sized cabinet where Edison could hide away to take a nap!

Edison believed he could make the telephone carry sound better. He went to work at his new laboratory, carrying out dozens of experiments with his staff. They tested how well different materials carried sound—everything from rubber to salt.

Menlo Park became a place full of energy, just like Thomas Edison. Between periods of quiet work, Edison rushed from one table to another to see what his workers were doing. He gave advice, told jokes, and spat tobacco juice on the floor.

The staff at the Menlo Park factory spent long hours working on Edison's ideas. For fun, they formed a band and kept a pet bear.

Work always came first, though. After months of effort, Edison solved the telephone puzzle in 1877. Adding two button-shaped pieces of carbon soot inside Bell's telephone made it carry sounds farther and more clearly.

Edison's carbon buttons made the telephone more than just an amazing machine. It worked well enough for people to use in their homes and businesses. At age thirty, Edison had the world talking in a whole new way.

The telephone, with Edison's improvements, became popular for business and even in homes.

3 THE SOUND OF SUCCESS

Edison liked to work on many new inventions at once. Whenever he got tired of one, he could switch to another. As he worked on his carbon telephone buttons, another idea was dancing in his head. He wanted to find a way to record a person's voice and play it back.

Edison made this drawing in his notebook showing how he planned to record the human voice.

Between telephone experiments, Edison worked on his new idea. He started by making gadgets with a telephone part called a diaphragm. A diaphragm is a thin metal disc that moves in response to a speaker's voice, helping a telephone carry sound.

When Edison attached a needle to a diaphragm, both objects moved with the speaker's voice. The needle could carve marks into a sheet of waxed paper. Tinfoil held the marks even better, he found.

The workers at Menlo Park made this talking machine based on Edison's drawing.

He was sure that those
simple marks were the key to
recording a voice. He had to figure out how
to turn them back into sound. Tom worked
for weeks, testing ideas and talking with
his Menlo Park staff. Finally he gave his
machine builder a new set of plans.

Edison's machine had a piece of tinfoil
wrapped around a cylinder—an object
shaped like a can. To make a recording, a
person turned a crank while speaking. The
speaker's voice moved a diaphragm, which
moved a needle. The needle recorded the
sound movements in the foil.

To play back the sound, the crank was turned again. A second needle moved over the tinfoil recording. The sounds that came out were exactly like those that had been spoken into the machine!

Edison called his new invention the phonograph. Like Bell's first telephone, it didn't work well enough yet for people to use in their homes. Still, no one had ever been able to record a human voice before.

The phonograph made Edison famous. Newspaper reporters nicknamed him the Wizard. All through 1878, people took the train to Menlo Park to meet him.

Edison (RIGHT) and one of his workers showed their phonograph to scientists in Washington, D.C.

Some were surprised by what they found. Edison rarely combed his hair, and his clothes were often dirty. He still spat tobacco juice as he talked.

Even though he seemed odd, he charmed visitors by showing off his "baby," the phonograph. He even let them make their own recordings.

That September, a reporter got the scoop on Thomas Edison's newest big idea. In just six weeks, Edison promised, he would light up a whole section of New York City—with electricity.

A Foolish Claim

In 1878, an amazing headline appeared in a New York newspaper. It boasted, "Edison Invents a Machine That Will Feed the Human Race—[Making] Biscuits, Meat, Vegetables, and Wine out of Air, Water, and Common Earth." Was Edison that good at inventing? Not quite. The headline appeared on April 1. It was an April Fool's Day joke!

FOOD -O- RAMIC

4 THE BRIGHTEST IDEA

Homes didn't have electricity in 1878. Street lamps and indoor lights burned natural gas, which was carried from place to place in underground pipes. Gas lamps were dirty and smelly—and sometimes they exploded.

Edison had to build a power station in New York City to make the electricity to light his electric light bulbs.

Electricity was the answer, Edison thought. A glass bulb built the right way ought to be able to give off light created by electricity. Many other inventors wanted to create such a light, too.

Two problems had to be solved for electric lighting to work. First, how could electricity be sent to thousands of different buildings at one time? Edison imagined a power station—a building with machines that would create a huge amount of electricity. Wires would carry the electricity wherever it was needed.

The second problem was the bulb itself. Other scientists had found that running electricity through a wire could make it glow and produce light. But the wire burned out within minutes. Edison needed to find a material that would burn for days.

While he and his crew worked on these problems, his son William was born in October 1878. Edison had little time to welcome the new baby.

As days went by, Edison realized that he had spoken too quickly when he promised electric lights in six weeks. It turned out that the first bulbs weren't ready to be shown to the public until the end of 1879.

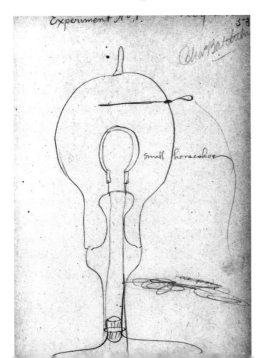

Edison drew this messy sketch to show how his lightbulb might work.

The first light bulb had a horseshoe-shaped bit of carbon-coated paper that could glow for hours.

Each bulb contained a horseshoe-shaped scrap of paper covered with carbon soot, the same material that Edison had used to improve the telephone. To the delight of the crowds that swarmed into Menlo Park, the bulbs burned with a pleasing glow that lasted for hours.

Still more months of work went by before the lighting system was ready to move from laboratory to city. Edison realized that he needed to be in New York City, to get the job done. In 1881, he moved his family there and opened a new lab.

At last, the electric wires Edison had imagined were laid underground through the streets of New York. Construction began on America's first power station. The only dim spot in Edison's excitement was that Mary seemed to be sick all the time. In 1882, her doctor suggested a vacation for the couple, but Edison couldn't leave his work. He sent Mary away on her own.

That September, the moment Edison had worked for came. His electric lights went on in New York City—and they worked!

Workers dug trenches in New York City to lay the electric wires for the new lighting system.

Edison had done more than invent a lightbulb. He had created a system for sending the power of electricity throughout a city. His success made him more famous than ever. Other cities built power stations. Edison's electric light company grew and grew. And he finally went on vacation with Mary, to Florida.

Sadly, one vacation wasn't enough to heal years of illness for Mary. She died in 1884, as Edison sobbed at her bedside. At at age thirty-seven, he was left with three children to raise.

ANOTHER BRIGHT IDEA

The lightbulb brightened more than streets and homes. Edward Johnson, one of Edison's assistants, created the first electric Christmas lights in 1882. Johnson strung eighty walnut-sized bulbs on the Christmas tree in his parlor. What color were the first Christmas lights? Red, white, and blue!

5 MOVIES AND MUSIC

It was a relief for Edison to go back to work a few weeks after Mary's death. He distracted himself from his sadness by making deals to expand electric lighting into new areas.

After Mary died, Edison married Mina Miller in 1886.

He soon realized that work alone didn't make him happy. In 1885, he met a dark-haired beauty named Mina Miller. Suddenly the Wizard was in love. "Got thinking about Mina," he wrote in his diary one day, "and came near to being run over by a street car."

Edison was thrilled to find that Mina liked him, too. He taught her Morse code so that they could tap quiet messages into one another's hands. One day, during a carriage ride, he tapped out a question. Would she marry him? "Yes," she tapped in reply.

After their wedding in 1886, the couple moved to Glenmont, an estate in West Orange, New Jersey. Edison built a new lab across from his house, much bigger than the one at Menlo Park.

Glenmont became the home of another Edison, Madeleine, who was born in 1888. By then, a new idea had taken hold in Edison's mind. He had already discovered how to record sounds with the phonograph. Now he wanted to make movies by recording movement on film.

Glenmont was an estate in West Orange, New Jersey. Edison bought it and moved his family there in 1886.

Eadweard Muybridge took many photographs in a series to show animals in motion.

In this new project, Edison found the ideas of other inventors especially helpful. Eadweard Muybridge had built a machine that held many photographs of a moving animal. The machine projected the photographs onto a screen one at a time, very rapidly. The animal on the screen appeared to move. But the movement was jerky and awkward.

Edison thought he could do better. He put a photography expert, William Dickson, on the job. Then Edison talked with an inventor who had built a device that took many pictures on a single, long strip of film.

This idea of a single film strip was what Dickson needed. It still took him two more years to work out the mechanical details. In the meantime, Edison's fifth child, Charles, was born in 1890.

In 1891, the movie machine worked at last. Edison called it a kinetoscope. It looked like a cabinet with a peephole built in. The viewer peered through the peephole to see a stream of photographs flow past. The photos flowed so quickly and smoothly that the movement they showed looked real.

Viewers looked into Edison's kinetoscope to see the first moving pictures.

Edison added a movie studio to the West Orange laboratory. By 1894, Americans could watch kinetoscope movies for a nickel each. The first ones were just a few minutes long, but people loved them. It was worth five cents to watch trained bears dancing, boxers throwing punches, and dancers kicking up their heels.

A movie studio was added to the West Orange factory to make the kinetoscope movies.

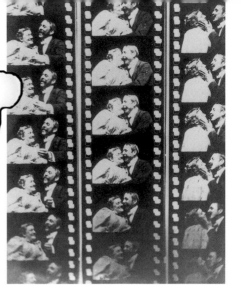

This series of single photos became the first movie kiss when shown in the kinetoscope.

Once his movie machine was making money, Edison turned back to an old favorite, the phonograph. He and his inventing team worked on making it less bulky and expensive. By 1899, a lightweight Edison phonograph called the Gem sold for ten dollars. At that price, any family with a little money to spare could enjoy music at home.

As always, Edison was busy with a new invention even as he finished the one before it. This time he had been inspired by the automobile, which came to America's streets during the 1890s. He noticed that the gasoline engines that powered cars were dirty and smelly. He began to work on a battery that could store enough clean, safe electricity to power a car.

The inventor's years of hard work were beginning to take a toll on his health. In 1907, he turned sixty years old. He began to spend more time away from the laboratory. In the winter, he took Mina and their three children to Florida.

Edison's car batteries were ready for the road in 1910. Cars that used them never had to fill up at the gas station, and they didn't create smoke or dirt. But most people were happy with gasoline cars, which cost less money.

For a while, Edison stayed almost as busy as ever. When the United States entered World War I in 1917, he worked on invention ideas for the navy. In 1927, he began studying new ways to make rubber.

Edison and his son Theodore, born in 1898, ride in a car powered by an electric battery.

HOLIDAY FUN

No matter how busy Edison was, he made sure to be home every Fourth of July. He woke Madeleine, Charles, and Theodore at the crack of dawn to set off firecrackers. Edison liked to make the children dance by tossing firecrackers at their feet! But he always gave the young Edisons a chance to make him dance as well.

At eighty years old, he liked to tell his admirers that he would still be working on the day he died. But those who knew him well could see that he was growing frail.

Thomas Edison died in 1931. He was buried in West Orange on October 21. That night, people all over America turned off their lights for one minute. With darkness, they honored the man who gave the world a lifetime of bright ideas.

TIMELINE

THOMAS EDISON
WAS BORN ON
FEBRUARY 11, 1847.

In the year . . .

1859　He got a job selling newspapers on trains.

1862　He became a telegraph operator. Age 15

1867　He built an electric vote recorder.

1869　He became a full-time inventor. Age 22

1871　He married Mary Stilwell.

1873　His daughter Marion, the first of his six children, was born.

1876　He opened a laboratory in Menlo Park, NJ. His son Thomas Alva Jr. was born.

1877　His son William Leslie was born. He invented a carbon button for telephones.

1878　He invented the phonograph. Age 31

1879　He invented the lightbulb.

1882　He opened the first power plant and lit part of New York City with lightbulbs.

1884　Mary died.

1886　He married Mina Miller and moved to West Orange, NJ.

1887　He built a new lab in West Orange.

1888　His daughter Madeleine was born.

1890　His son Charles was born.

1891　He invented a machine that showed movies. Age 44

1898　His son Theodore was born.

1910　He invented an electric car battery.

1917　He worked on ideas for the United States Navy.

1927　He worked on new ways to make rubber.

1931　He died in West Orange on October 18. Age 84

THE HOUSE THAT TOM BUILT

Not all of Edison's inventions became famous. One remarkable idea that didn't quite catch on was the cement house. Cement is a liquid that becomes hard like stone when it dries. It's often used to build basements and sidewalks. Edison thought that cement could be used to build entire houses. He built a hollow frame, called a mold, in the shape of a house. Cement was poured into the mold and allowed to dry. When the mold was taken apart, the cement house needed nothing but doors and windows. Edison built a few cement houses for his workers, but most people didn't find his idea very appealing.

The poured cement houses that Edison invented never became popular.

FURTHER READING

Branley, Franklin M. *Day Light, Night Light: Where Light Comes From.* **New York: HarperCollins, 1998.** What happens inside a lightbulb? This book explains the science of Edison's invention and other kinds of light.

Cottringer, Anne. *Movie Magic.* **New York: DK Publishing, 1999.** Find out how modern movies are filmed, including camerawork and special effects.

Harper, Cherise Mericle. *Imaginative Inventions: The Who, What, Where, When, and Why of Roller Skates, Potato Chips, Marbles, and Pie (and More!).* **New York: Little, Brown, 2001.** This rhyming picture book tells the story of many inventions we use every day.

Sherrow, Victoria. *Alexander Graham Bell.* **Minneapolis: Carolrhoda Books, 2001.** The story of another great inventor—the man who beat Edison in the race to invent the telephone.

WEBSITES

Edison Birthplace Museum
<http://www.tomedison.org> Visitors to this site can view photographs of the room where Edison was born and learn about his early years in Milan, Ohio.

Edison's Miracle of Light
<http://www.pbs.org/wgbh/amex/edison/> This public-television website features recordings made by Edison's company, photographs, a timeline of the inventor's life, and details about the creation of the lightbulb.

Edison National Historic Site
<http://www.nps.gov/edis/home.htm> View a family photo album and learn about Edison's inventing process at the website of his home and laboratory in West Orange, New Jersey.

Edison: The Wizard of Menlo Park
<http://www.edisonnj.org/menlopark/taemenlo.asp> This huge website includes information about the Menlo Park laboratory and the many things Edison invented there.

SELECT BIBLIOGRAPHY

Baldwin, Neil. *Edison: Inventing the Century.* New York: Hyperion, 1995.

Clark, Ronald W. Edison: *The Man Who Made the Future.* New York: G. P. Putnam's Sons, 1977.

Israel, Paul. *Edison: A Life of Invention.* New York: John Wiley and Sons, 1998.

Josephson, Matthew. *Edison: A Biography.* New York: McGraw-Hill, 1959.

Wachhorst, Wyn. *Thomas Alva Edison: An American Myth.* Cambridge, MA: MIT Press, 1981.

INDEX

Acknowledgments

For photographs and artwork: U.S. Department of the Interior, National Parks Service, Edison National Historic Site, pp. 4, 7, 10, 11, 13, 15, 16, 17, 18, 19, 22, 23, 25, 26, 27, 30, 31, 33, 36, 37, 39, 40, 41, 45; © Bettmann/CORBIS, pp. 8, 32; © CORBIS, p. 9; American Dictionary of Portraits, p. 20; © Hulton|Archive by Getty Pictures, p. 38; Underwood & Underwood, p. 42. Cover images by U.S. Department of the Interior, National Parks Service, Edison National Historic Site (front and back).
For quoted material: p. 28, Wachhorst, Wyn. *Thomas Alva Edison: An American Myth.* Cambridge, MA: MIT Press, 1981; p. 36, from Thomas Edison's journal, quoted in Baldwin, Neil. *Edison: Inventing the Century.* New York: Hyperion, 1995.